GW00640711

*The God Beyond
Tradition*

The God Beyond Tradition

Stephen Shaw

Acknowledgements

My special thanks to my wife, Promilla for her constant support, encouragement, and wonderful artwork; and also to those who have worked in detail with me on this project; my father, Keith; my cousin, Brian Campbell; and friends, Murt O'Brien, Ann Lysaght, and Martin Mulchrone.

And with thanks to so many others who have read the book and passed comments, all of which have in some way been invaluable.

I am also indebted to Peter Goldman for his kind introduction, and to David Norris, Lilla Bek, Maura Lundberg and Peter Gill for their reviews.

Biographical Note

Stephen Shaw was born in 1949. His original training was in Computer Science – a Programmer/Systems Analyst for twelve years. He has been working in the field of Alternative Medicine since qualifying as a Spinologist in 1984, as an Acupuncturist in 1991, and as a Chinese Herbalist in 1994.

He has practised meditation in a variety of forms since 1975, and taken part in many self development courses.

He first met Promilla in December 1991 in Delhi Airport after a month travelling India. They were married a year later, and now live in Dublin with their daughter Emily.

Dedicated to Emily

Contents

Preface

In the age to come, practising the presence of God, meditation and a conscious awareness of the living moment may very well be part of normal education and of daily life. In times past, these disciplines were basic to religious and spiritual practice and initiation training. Nowadays, as we approach the millennium it is for us as individuals to voluntarily choose to investigate these paths.

Technological growth creates spiritual hunger. At some point the containment of religious tradition releases the devotee into the freedom of its universal spiritual mystery.

In our search, the finest guide is where another's personal experience speaks as if directly to each one of us. This is when a book becomes a special friend. The ideas become a personal conversation between the author and ourself. As we read, our questions are answered, our thoughts discussed. The author's journey as our reference feels genuine and relevant. It becomes like our inner voice.

Stephen Shaw writes from long and broad experience. He has sifted through so much on his own way and he offers what he really practices.

This is a book to be read many times. Each time we will discover another perspective within ourself. It is a book to remind us gently and insistently when we have lapsed that it's alright to begin again right now. Whatever the situation or location, we know we can remain present, centred, in touch with the God within; and that it is possible to live life fully and deeply.

These are ideas to take on a journey, expressed simply and clearly; ageless tools relevant more than ever in these times.

Peter Goldman
21st January 1997

The God Beyond Tradition

Introduction

The very notion of God as an experience, beyond the traditional "Something Out There", will for many be an alien concept. The purpose of this book is to bring an understanding to that concept, and to help the experience of God become a reality for those who desire it. There is an increasing number of people dissatisfied with the answers provided by mainstream religions. No longer is it acceptable to be told to have faith, that God is a mystery which one does not question. It is firstly to these people searching for answers to such basic questions as "Who or what is God?" and "How does God become a practical reality in my life?" that this book is directed; secondly to those already treading a pathway towards inner knowledge and looking for ways to broaden their experience.

Time spent in the field must serve as my credentials for writing this book, since I have no allegiance to any religious or spiritual organisation which might confer some label of respectability. I have spent the best part of my life looking for ways to find God, or at least what my interpretation of God happened to be at each step along the way. The reason for the search was simply a belief that in the long term it would make me happier, coupled with a burning curiosity about the mysteries of life. My spiritual journey is far from over, but in recent years I am happy to say that I have seen tangible results from my efforts. It is these results that have inspired this attempt to communicate some of the insights and methods of practice which have led to my experience of inner change.

My first memories of a spiritual search go back to my secondary boarding school; a Protestant school with a chapel which we had to attend twice daily. Lost and unhappy at this strange place, I naturally turned to my religion for solace. I remember watching everyone attending the religious services, reading the Bible and praying regularly week by week, year by year. Somewhere through all this I heard some of Christ's message and kept wondering, "If this is what it takes to get into heaven and this Saviour has come to earth to give us his message, then why is everyone going to church to pray, yet no one is putting these teachings into practice with any real conviction?"

As my feelings of loneliness diminished over some time, so also did my religious phase pass into the background of various school activities. When I was about sixteen a group of us discovered that you could contact "spirits" by each one putting a finger on a glass with the alphabet spread on a table. When someone asked a question the glass would move to the relevant letters and spell out the answer. We surprised many of our school friends one Saturday by predicting the score of the international rugby match after a hot tip from our glass. During the time of these seances, which took place over the course of many months, we were all convinced that we were in touch with the spirit world, so that for us it became a living reality. At this stage the subject of reincarnation was raised, and our "glass spirit" told us that we had each lived before several times. The notion that we were each on a pathway towards some sort of spiritual perfection, and that the state of being attained in one lifetime could be carried forward into the next, appealed to me. It seemed to answer a lot of the riddles concerning the injustices in the world. I began to read books on the subject. The perfect state of "Nirvana" which we were all supposed to be gradually moving towards was said to take tens of lifetimes to reach, but with great effort and dedication it was thought to be possible for a person to make the journey in just one lifetime. So it occurred to me that it must surely be worthwhile to make a big effort to get there this time round rather than waste several more lifetimes in the cycle of death and rebirth.

Once again the now revised spiritual quest receded into the background as I left school and entered the big wide world with its new set of attractions and pressures. But the seeds had been sown, and although with the arrogance of youth I thought that I had my life pretty well worked out, something told me I would one day return to those ideas which had taken root during my schooldays, and develop them further.

When I was twenty-five I met a young lady whose apparent inner calm impressed me a great deal. She seemed to have something I did not possess - a natural sense of well-being without having to resort to external stimuli - and I was anxious to get in on the act. She had for the past two years been practising Transcendental Meditation, so I made up my mind that I would learn this technique to try and improve my own state of well-being. I subsequently learned how to meditate, and have since been doing so regularly for more than twenty years. I have found this practice very beneficial. It has made me healthier, calmer and more able to communicate. Additionally it has eliminated the need for such props as alcohol and cigarettes to make life bearable. Even the inevitability of death, which in the past has haunted me from time to time, no longer instils a sense of dread. This may be because the process of letting go which occurs in meditation is a very beautiful experience, and I find it easy to conceive of death as a similar form of release into a more joyful state of being. I could list many other changes, but one which stands above the rest is that it has put me in contact with a part of myself which is able to look at things from a different perspective - one centred in stillness. I seem now to have more of an aerial view of the events taking place in my life, and a greater sense of clarity. That still part of myself which I contact in meditation is, I believe, the same as is referred to by many different names, including the Higher Self, Pure Consciousness, the Infinite Spirit, and also as God.

Inherent in the philosophy of Transcendental Meditation was the premise that as one meditated the stress which had accrued in mind and body would gradually diminish. Hand in hand with this process one would become progressively more in touch with the Higher Self until a state of "Cosmic Consciousness" was reached. At this point virtually all stress and tension would be gone, leaving one in a state of permanent bliss. To achieve this, all one had to do was meditate twice a day for twenty minutes, live a normal life and the rest would take care of itself. This I believed, and continued in this way of thinking for many years with little deviation from the basic rule of practice. As already stated, I was receiving profound benefits, but time was passing and the much desired state of Cosmic Consciousness never seemed much closer than the distant horizon. I could recognise contact with the Higher Consciousness to varying degrees each time I meditated, but in daily life I was still having my ups and downs, even if now to a lesser extent.

Frustrated by the slowness of pace towards my goal of enlightenment I explored concepts from other teachers. I read books, listened to tapes, attended lectures and talked to friends of like mind in the hope of finding a means of acceleration.

Then, quite recently, a message I had been hearing on and off for years from various sources finally got through to me. It is essentially this: that God is Life, not something to be found at some distant time, but a reality to be experienced *Here and Now*. All we have to do is let go of our constant need to analyse and automatically we start to come into this Eternal Presence. You may think "Easier said than done", but I can confirm that the practice of a few routine exercises does bring results. Through such exercises and over a period of time, I have experienced some of that Presence as a part of my daily life in a tangible way, rather than making contact at meditation time only.

The people I am hoping to reach with this book fall broadly into two categories: firstly, those just beginning the search for a concept of God they can make real for themselves: secondly, those who have already been on a spiritual pathway for some time, and would like to bring that consciousness experienced in meditation into the rest of their lives. Those in the first category may find some chapters seem complicated, while those in the second may find certain sections simplistic. This is the dilemma in trying to cater to a broad spectrum of people, but the hope is to avoid excluding potential readers.

I have referred to the Christian Bible on a few occasions, not because I adhere to this more than to other traditions, but because firstly I am more familiar with it, and secondly experience has led me to expect more opposition from Christians than from others.

I hope there are people somewhere who may be helped by the methods I endeavour to describe, towards experiencing the Presence of God in a more direct way. I realise this will not be the correct path for everyone. Some will not yet be ready for it, others will have already developed beyond the need for it: still more are travelling on equally valid but parallel pathways. The methods have enabled me to open a door within to a deeper spiritual awareness. I hope to be able to point out that door to others, who are looking for a means to accelerate their progress along the path to self realisation.

What Do We Mean By God?

How does one begin to define the indefinable? When I ask people what their concept of God is, I always seem to get a different answer; perhaps one indication that the very nature of God is indeed outside the realm of definition. Yet if we are to use this term which is the subject of such controversy, there must be some common understanding of what we mean by the word. People often tend to externalise God as some sort of benevolent personality in a kind of vague human form if not exactly our traditional "Man with the Beard". They get confused because He is supposed to be all powerful and all loving, yet allows extremes of misery to exist in the world.

We may get less bogged down by these issues if we can see God not so much as an individual personality but more as the force of love, intelligence or consciousness itself; a kind of potential source of energy for us to tap into or not as we choose. This could be likened to the electricity in our house: it's always there and available but we will never see a sign of it unless we plug in our gadget and switch it on.

My understanding of God, which is far from absolute, comes from my experience combined with the teachings I feel most comfortable with. It is as follows:

Everything we can see or touch or feel or in any external sense identify is not God as such, but the manifest world, i.e. the world of form. God is that which we cannot see, touch or feel. It is the Great Void, unmanifest and formless, which permeates the world of form. The nature of this formlessness is pure Consciousness, pure Intelligence and pure Love.

It may be easier to understand this phenomenon if one can imagine a time before Creation when the Great Void existed alone. Within this Void was the seed of the Universe, but solely as potential, still unmanifest. The tendency for vibration to occur within this Sea of Potential was the very beginning of form arising out of formlessness. It is perhaps this vibration or sound that the Bible refers to in its verse: "In the beginning was the Word, and the Word was with God, and the Word was God" (St. John 1:1).

The earlier and more refined stages of vibration may have begun to form what some people term the "Spirit World" before becoming gradually more coarsened into the dense world of matter. But all of creation was still permeated by the Great Void, hence "The Kingdom of God is within" (St. Luke 17:21).

Before and after the world of form was created, the Great Void (or God) exists only in the Eternal Now and therefore has no sense of past or future. In order to be in contact with God, therefore, one must come into *Present Time Consciousness.*

To live in the present is simply just to *Be.* God is sometimes described as the *"Great I Am".* When you experience *"I Am"* as a pure state of being, as opposed to the usual qualifications of "I am hungry, sad, fed up, excited etc.", then you experience God or Consciousness in its pure state for whatever

period of time you can maintain it. Incidentally "Jehova", the word for God sometimes used in the Bible, is actually an Aramaic word meaning "I am".

In the Old Testament there is a famous quotation "Be still and know that I Am God" (Psalms 46:10). This experience of *"I Am"* in its purest state, the knowing that *"I Am God"*, is the natural state that we were designed to live in for most of the time, but which we have for some reason lost touch with. It was said that "In order to enter the Kingdom of Heaven you must become as a little child". A child knows God because it knows how to just *"Be"* - in fact it doesn't know anything else. It has not yet learned to put concepts or definitions on things, therefore is still seeing the world at first hand. It lives mainly in the present because it seldom thinks, at least not in a rational sense. It is contented to enjoy the sensations of just being, *Here and Now*. Entering "The Kingdom", which is not restricted to a time beyond this life, requires that in some way we regress to this natural childlike state.

When the new world of form was created out of the Great Void, then began the relative reality of time and space. The Great Void is eternal and simultaneously everywhere, therefore knows no time or space limitations. By contrast matter occupies an area of space and exists for a limited time.

We as humans have the capacity to identify ourselves with God by living in the present or to identify ourselves with form by living in a world of past and future oriented thinking. It is the overuse of our rational minds that keeps us locked into the worlds of form for most of our lives.

In actual fact we have access to two minds, our rational mind and our God Mind, or Higher Mind. Our rational mind, which is the one that we are used to thinking with, works relatively slowly by drawing comparisons and computing results. The Higher Mind works infinitely more rapidly, by intuition, bringing to us virtually instantaneously the optimal response to any situation at any given time. Although we in our present condition have little contact with it, we can see it in operation sometimes when we have a "gut response" to some problem or when we are relaxing and suddenly find inspiration coming to us from apparently nowhere. It sounds rather like magic, but the Higher Mind may in fact use the same logical pathways as the rational mind. It is just that we cannot identify it because it operates subconsciously.

In our natural state we should be able to relax and let go of the rational mind, allowing the Higher Mind take over most tasks much in the same way as we let our autonomic mind take over when we drive a car or tie our shoe laces. Our rational mind has its occasional uses, for instance where time schedules have to be adhered to, but its function should be secondary to the Higher Mind rather than the virtual monopoly which it is currently holding.

In order to give a more practical meaning to these words, and as a prelude to learning to meditate, there follows a short exercise which may be practised at any convenient moment to increase your contact with the Source of Life:

Exercise to Contact the Source

Sit in a comfortable chair. Close your eyes. Keeping your attention present, look inside and see what you can feel. At first you will probably notice the darkness. Then you may feel some discomfort in the body, for instance around the solar plexus area. This is coming from past thoughts and emotions. Breathe into the discomfort and feel it lessen to some degree. Now look inside again and notice if you can feel some good feeling there somewhere, even alongside the remaining discomfort. The good feeling may take the form of a sense of some warmth or clarity. This pleasant feeling is the *Life* inside you; it is always there to be found. Since *God Is Life* then simply know that you have contacted God within you. This is not some mythical God, but the Living God that can be experienced *Here and Now* - any time, any place.

Benefits of Maintaining Contact

To keep up the practice of exercises such as this requires a certain commitment, especially at times when results might seem slow to come. It is important, therefore, to understand just what can be gained from contact with the Higher Consciousness. Three of the major benefits are:

Firstly, through the intuition, we are provided with a guidance system (described earlier) helping us at all times to fulfil our ongoing requirements.

Secondly, by acting from this level of consciousness we are spontaneously acting in harmony with the laws of nature and are therefore in turn supported by nature. This means simply that the conditions in our lives improve. (On the veracity of this law, the traditions are unanimous, from the Christian "As you sow, so shall you reap" to the Eastern Karmic Laws of cause and effect.)

Thirdly, by becoming one with this source of creation we are automatically filled with Its nature, that of Love and Bliss - so we experience these qualities in the form of self-healing, regeneration, good feelings and a general love of Creation in Its manifold expressions.

Depletion Caused by the Rational Mind

By contrast, the rational or lower mind which we are currently using to excess, is constantly depleting our energies in a number of ways:

In the first place, thinking in this way stimulates our emotions, usually fear related ones which are energy draining, often irrational, and primarily responsible for all human conflict, both internal and external.

In the second place, the rational mind works by referring to a set of definitions that we have been accumulating into our memories since birth – a kind of library of all our experiences. These definitions are essential to our survival and stability – without them we would be like "babes in the wilderness", with no point of reference. In that light definitions would seem purely beneficial, but there is a problem: we use them far too often. Even a walk in the country which should be a pleasurable experience of being in the senses, for most of us is largely spent in analysing past or future scenarios. The smell of a rose is more potent when one is just breathing in the fragrance, rather than trying to figure out which type of rose it is. The more analysis we do, the more we crowd out the senses – our prime link to reality. Another drawback of definitions is that they themselves often become outdated. In other words the images that used to frighten us as children no longer have the same relevance when we become adults. Yet these old definitions still haunt us. So we sometimes find ourselves responding irrationally to some situation which has triggered a fear in us associated with the distant past. A common example of this is the fear many people have of authority figures. To compound the above features, referring to definitions with the rational mind is, in contrast to the intuition, a slow and tiring form of mental activity: it is like a car struggling in first gear along a highway where fourth gear would have been so much more efficient.

In the third place, depletion of energy occurs because the very use of the thinking or rational mind creates a filter over the screen of consciousness, thereby depriving one of the life giving energies being constantly supplied by the Source of Creation. This can be likened to a cloud in the sky which obstructs the sun's rays from reaching the earth. In this analogy, the sun is the Source of Creation, the earth our screen of consciousness, and clouds are thoughts. In our natural state where the rational mind is only occasionally used, we should have a blue sky with the occasional puffy white cloud, providing a little variety to a sunny day. However, the picture one might see for the vast majority of people today would be a sky almost totally clouded over with thick grey clouds and bursts of rain with occasional thunder. These clouds, which represent our past thoughts and emotions, have been building up for countless years and hang around us, blocking out the pure light of consciousness, dulling our minds and triggering a sense of dread when problems present themselves. Even when we stop activity and sit quietly inactive, that sense of dread seems to lurk there as a vague discomfort in the body, giving us the feeling that all is not well.

Balancing Between Two Worlds

It is important to realise that we inhabit two interpenetrating worlds with highly contrasting natures. When we identify with one of these worlds, we abide in the Eternal One, and are linked to all of creation. When we identify with the other, we view things from the individual standpoint. Both modes are valid, and we have been designed with the capacity to switch alternately between both of these worlds. Ideally, from the inner peace and stillness of the Higher Self we dip into the rational mind from time to time, but return always to the stillness, our true home.

If we wish to redress the imbalance which has occurred, then we must begin to shift the emphasis from our lower rational mind to our Higher God Mind. Therein lies the key to fulfilment.

Where Did We Go Wrong?

Nobody could say that mankind as a whole has really shown itself to be very enlightened or life supporting over recent years or even centuries. We have made war regularly on each other and have in general treated our fellow humans rather poorly, not to mention the degradation we have caused our planet as soon as advancing technology gave us the opportunity.

If we were designed with the capacity to live our lives centred in the Divine Consciousness, then how did it come about that we are now living in such a low state of awareness? How could we have sacrificed a heritage of inner bliss and harmony for lives of tension and discontent tempered only by the occasional brief respite, which somehow manages to preserve the feeling that life is worth living?

Some of the legends of varying traditions tell of a golden age in our distant past when a state of harmony prevailed in the world. The story of Adam and Eve in the Bible has been interpreted in different ways. I like to view it as a metaphor for the first men and women to inhabit the earth, rather than take it as literally meaning the first man and woman (incidentally the Hebrew word Adam means "Mankind", while Eve means "Womankind"). The Garden of Eden they inhabited thus represents the state of consciousness of men and women in those early times. They were at that time governed by their higher intuitive minds because their rational minds had not yet learned to dominate their thinking processes. They were a little like children, enjoying the fruits of the garden without questioning how they got there. And so they had God's blessing to enjoy the many experiences the world had to offer in whatever manner they pleased, save for one exception: they must not eat the fruit from the "Tree of the Knowledge of Good and Evil". Seeking knowledge of good and evil is a function of the rational mind. Unlike the Higher Mind, which functions on a spontaneous intuitive response level, the rational mind wants to know everything in detail about its environment so that it can build a framework of reference in which to live. Mankind in God Consciousness knew intuitively that pursuing the analytical thought processes which allow judgement of relative rights and wrongs through deduction would begin a slippery slope that would gradually lead to his being cut off from the Source of Being. He was tempted by the "Serpent" of curiosity, against the advice of his intuition, into a process of clouding the consciousness with judgements, concepts and the inevitable accompanying patterns of fear related emotions so that, perhaps after many centuries, the Light of God dimmed to the extent that we experience today.

It may be that one of the tasks of our being on earth is to explore the rational mind and gradually bring it under the control of the Higher Mind, but at that stage of our evolution we were not ready for such an undertaking.

And so the centuries and millennia passed while we developed increasingly sophisticated

defence mechanisms to protect what we now call the ego, the "I" of the lower self. This is the "I" that imagines itself to be separate, as opposed to the "I" of the One Source that is linked to all other "I"s.

In this long intervening period great spiritual teachers have come and gone. All have tried to free us from the chains of bondage forged by our analytical minds. Occasionally one or another has lived the message taught by the master and experienced freedom. But mostly we have talked about it, argued about it, fought over it and bored each other with it, forever creating more clouds of rational thinking to blur our consciousness even further.

The religions have played the worst part because they claimed to be able to lead people towards God. Not only did they largely fail in that aspiration, but through the false sense of security they gave people, in convincing them that performing certain rituals would lead them to salvation, they took away the inclination for people to seek out the truth for themselves. In short, religions have distracted people from the truth by over complication. There is a part in all of us that seeks spiritual truth and freedom - the part that knows we should be living more fulfilled lives. If that part of us pokes its head out, asks a few questions, and in return finds a mass of verbiage and confusion, it may well label its package of questions as "unsolvable mysteries to be looked at another time", and retreat back into its protective shell. This has happened for too many who have taken the trouble to look for truth in a small way at some point in their lives.

The majority of people in the West now broadly fall into three categories:

Firstly, those totally committed to a belief system, who follow it blindly to the letter without ever questioning its validity. Secondly, those who believe there is probably "Something Out There", and half-heartedly follow the tradition they were brought up in, hoping that if a day of judgement ever comes, they will not be judged harshly. Thirdly, those who don't know if there is a God and don't believe it is worth the effort of trying to find out, or else simply believe there is no God.

There are many who believe, and I tend to share this optimistic view, that we are moving towards a more enlightened period in the earth's history. If it is true, then this new age will be ushered in by those who have already begun the journey back to an awareness of the Divine Presence within, for they will be affecting others both by example and on a vibrational level. In recent years there appears to be a polarisation taking place between life supporting and destructive elements in society. Crime has been rising, its nature becoming increasingly savage, internal struggles within countries have intensified, and general stress levels seem to be at an all time high. On the other hand, there has been a definite shift of many people towards more positive or spiritually based ways of living. This has manifested in a variety of ways, some examples being: a growing tendency to treat disease as a manifestation of disharmony within the whole spiritual, mental, emotional and physical make-up of a person rather than viewing the body as a set of isolated body parts and systems; a greater response to the plight of the less fortunate nations; increasing ecological awareness; a releasing of the oppressive hold of communism; a drive by many to seek the Living Spirit within their religious system rather than to merely follow form. This polarisation, if taken to its logical conclusion may intensify to the point where we will all have to choose whether we are in the camp of the life supporters or destroyers as the boundaries become more clearly defined. As already stated, it is the lower rational mind which leads us into mental chaos, while the Higher Mind leads us towards harmony and coherence. Therefore the ultimate choice will be whether to cling to the old ways of attachment to established belief systems and concepts with accompanying fear motivated actions, or to enter the newness of the *Here and Now* where all motivation springs from love, since love is *Its* nature.

The choice should be an easy one for those who can honestly look at and evaluate the options, but it is one that will have to be constantly renewed. As will be demonstrated, entering the Divine Presence is easy; maintaining it requires more than a little perseverance. Beginning Here and Now seems as good a place and time to start as any.

The Journey Back

Having identified the problem - that is the lowered state of consciousness we have now reached, and some of the reasons why this has come about, we are now faced with the question of how best to leave our world of illusions behind and re-enter the state of full consciousness which is our rightful heritage.

We are living in a new age of technology, but also in what is termed, by many on a spiritual path, the "New Age", where methods for reaching enlightenment abound. These methods include literally hundreds of spiritual, psychological and physical techniques. So, how can a person beginning on this vitally important journey towards self realisation be sure he or she has found the right path, or even that the path being followed has any validity at all?

It is very easy in the search for God to be seduced by a system of thought that, through the use of a few key sentences, appeals to one's sense of logic. Salvation is offered if one will only observe certain prescribed practices. The pull is made stronger by the support of group members attached to the particular faith, who will always validate the teachings at every step along the way. On questioning the faith one may be given answers which seem logical on a superficial level, but yet are only partly satisfying. The force of the group here can make a big difference in convincing one of something that otherwise would have been unacceptable. In a very subtle and insidious way one may be led down pathways of thinking to conclusions which are simply untrue. For instance, I regard the Bible as being a book containing much wisdom that may be used from time to time to enhance or validate my spiritual understanding. From this perspective I can take what I need without any sense of restriction, leaving aside those parts which I either cannot understand or do not feel comfortable with. But the Bible has been subject to rigid interpretations by many sects over the years, and the argument is usually along these lines:

"The Bible is the word of God because such and such a passage (in the Bible) says so. The Bible has stood the test of thousands of years, and many of the Biblical prophesies have come true".

If these statements are accepted as a premise for believing that every word contained in the Bible is the absolute word of God, we are in danger of giving the authority for how we live our life over to a book. The danger is intensified if we take every word literally. There is a sect in America where the followers dance with poisonous snakes and many die from the bites they receive, because somewhere in the Bible it says "And thou shalt take up serpents". This can be the danger of rigid interpretation. When dealing with a book as old as the Bible, and written in a foreign language, one must keep in mind that certain parts may possibly have been less inspired by God than others, or that certain things said may have related to a particular context, or were meant metaphorically, or perhaps lost a little in the translation.

A disciple of the Lord Buddha, having been

led astray many times by different people, once asked the master whom he could believe. The answer was given "Believe nothing which any man says, not even I, unless it appeals to your common sense; and even then do not believe until such time as you can prove it for yourself". This would seem to be good advice.

The techniques suggested in this book do not require a belief in anything that cannot be demonstrated through experience. I do make the statement that God is to be experienced when you become yourself, and that means entering the Present Moment. I ask only that you suspend disbelief until you are able to verify this. Making contact with the Higher Self is not difficult, in fact we have all had moments when we were taken unawares by a sense of a deeper presence - perhaps when relaxing in a bath, watching a sunset, or listening to classical music. It may not have been dramatic - just a good feeling of being peaceful, present and clear. The task at hand is firstly to recognise the experience, then to find ways of bringing it about and finally, by increasing the number and duration of these experiences, to maintain them to the point where one's life becomes more centred in the Divine Consciousness than in the rational mind.

This last part requires a strong sense of purpose, and the commitment to be persistent in the practice of being in the *Here and Now.* A sense of purpose will come when the processes involved are understood and a realisation gained of what may be achieved from the standpoint of one's quality of life.

Patience is needed for this work, as results may take some time. We have taken a very long time to accumulate all of the negativity that is locked inside us, and it is not going to disappear overnight. It is rather like sweeping out a room full of dust; the room at first fills with clouds of dust but when that dust settles the room is cleaner. In a similar way, when we first open up to the light of our Higher Consciousness, we start a healing process in motion which releases stress and loosens the ego structures and boundaries, making us feel uncomfortable at times. But each time the dust clouds of the mind settle we become that much clearer inside.

The journey back to full consciousness involves two processes - entering the Divine Presence, and clearing away the clouds of our past thinking and emotions. "Clearing away the clouds" is usually necessary in order to enter the Divine Presence, and entering the Divine Presence tends to bring up more clouds of past thinking and emotions to the surface of the awareness. So these two processes can be seen to interact with each other.

The "clouds" we experience usually as a vague sense of discomfort in the body, quite often around the solar plexus, chest or throat areas. They manifest sometimes as a feeling that something is not quite right but we cannot quite put our finger on exactly what it is. Without realising it we are constantly avoiding coming in contact with these feelings. We do this by distracting ourselves in any number of ways, for instance by seeking entertainment. In a very subtle way we use our rational minds to distract ourselves from the feelings which have in fact been produced by our rational minds in the first place.

How do we overcome this vicious circle?

The key to this dilemma lies in the fact that some of our thoughts occur spontaneously while others we initiate by choice. Spontaneous thoughts we cannot control. They are part of a chain that we seem to be conscious of in retrospect, arising in response to the multitude of day to day happenings we experience.

Thoughts that we initiate occur in a different way. Often we may find ourselves thinking about something and then come to a gap in the thought process. In that gap we are briefly suspended in the Eternity of The Present – *a Moment of Self Awareness.* Instead of exploring that space between the thoughts, and holding the awareness, people will normally return to continue the same thought process or begin a new topic. Staying in the space seems to be a bit frightening, a sense of entering unknown territory and so there is a compulsion to enter once again the familiar ground of rational thinking. The thoughts we initiate ourselves we can actually stop by first observing when we are doing it and then by simply stopping thinking. Ironically you cannot try to stop thinking - trying is thinking. You simply recognise the point at which you are about to begin a thought process and then choose not to. It is just letting go. In fact it takes less effort not to think than it takes to think.

There are three reasons why we stay locked in our thoughts:

The first is habit. Thinking is familiar territory and we have got used to finding a new train of thought when the previous one has run its course, without being aware that we are doing it. We see rational thoughts as normal and natural, and many even think that our being conscious is dependent on having thoughts. In fact it is the opposite. The screen of consciousness shines brightest when there are no thoughts. It is like the light from a film projector. The screen is at its brightest when there is no film in the projector. As soon as any film is played the screen darkens. Similarly, consciousness is at its clearest and brightest when there are no thoughts to obstruct it.

The second reason is fear of the unknown. As soon as you stop thinking, there is an immediate expansion of consciousness - a feeling of all structures and boundaries disappearing. People are often afraid of this sensation, and may think they are losing their minds or going insane. In fact they are releasing their hold of the lower rational mind and allowing the higher intuitive mind to take over. But there is no reason to fear; on two counts - one, the Higher Mind is well able to take on all the functions assigned to it; and two, the lower mind is only too glad to reappear at the first impulse of fear, which is why it is difficult in the beginning stages of practice to stay in the present for more than a few seconds. And far from going insane, the very opposite is happening. In the process of entering the present moment one is beginning to come under the influence of the Higher God Mind which can only bring coherence and harmony.

The third factor that keeps us thinking is a desire to avoid pain or discomfort. The stresses and strains which have accumulated during our lifetime hang over us like a kind of etheric body, previously referred to as "clouds of past thinking and emotions". These "clouds" have accumulated in the first place either because of our inability to express our emotions or because we have not allowed ourselves to feel them. When we repress an emotion it stays locked inside us and remains so until it is finally experienced. The key to clearing away these uncomfortable feelings is through our conscious attention - that is through "feeling the feelings". This is the way they are dispersed. Normally we are constantly avoiding the discomfort of these feelings by using our thoughts to distract ourselves from them. For instance, if you are sitting in a waiting room you will invariably find that people entering will look for a magazine to read even if they have little interest in the contents, just in order to avoid the discomfort of being with themselves for a short while.

In the process of becoming conscious, such feelings of discomfort arise again and again, and each one has to be felt in order for it to be dispersed. It is actually not as unpleasant as it may sound. The discomfort that accompanies each feeling is not as great as the initial sensation would lead one to believe, and will normally disperse quite quickly, leaving behind an increased sense of peace and well-being.

The above descriptions may seem technical, but in order to put the techniques of entering Higher Consciousness into practice, it helps to be aware of the ways in which the rational mind can trick us into staying under its control.

The next two chapters describe techniques for expanding our link with the God within, firstly by way of meditation, and secondly through bringing our daily activity into the *Here and Now.*

Meditation

editation is to be found in all the major religions, although tending to be more widely practised in those of the East, such as the Hindu and Buddhist traditions. People take up meditation for a variety of reasons: the desire to be less tense; to sleep better; to be more healthy; to stop addictions such as smoking and drinking; to think more clearly and thereby manage life more effectively; to understand one's spiritual side more fully; and generally to be happier.

Meditation does improve all these areas of one's life, but indirectly, as a by product of entering a state of inner harmony and coherence. It is a way of withdrawing, for a period of time, from normal daily activity, and allowing the mind to come to rest in the Divine Consciousness. Some people view prayer as talking to God and meditation by comparison as listening to God. I prefer to see meditation as becoming *One* with God to the degree to which a person is capable at that particular time. As the mind settles and we become still inside, our focus gradually shifts from the world of form into the formless Presence of God. To the extent that we can enter this stillness, our mind becomes the Mind of God. It is not that the Mind of God is something that exists apart from us, but rather that we normally separate ourselves from it by the continual chattering of the rational mind.

There are many well established techniques of meditation, and no claim is made that the one presented here is better than any other: but there is a reason for presenting it. Most forms of meditation induce a state of relaxation by diverting the attention away from the mind to an object such as a candle, a word, or the rising and falling of the breath. They cannot easily be practised during daily activity as it then becomes necessary to perform two separate functions simultaneously, namely the meditation plus the activity. In this way the attention is always split between the two. For instance, if you are trying to do something, while at the same time also attempting to continuously repeat a word, the two activities will interfere with each other as the attention cannot be fully devoted to either.

The meditation described here can, on the other hand, be used during daily activity for the reason that it does not interfere with the attention. This is achieved through consciously feeling the feelings produced by the senses, and then allowing the attention to focus on whatever activity is taking place. Through this *Allowing* of the attention to just *Be,* coupled with the conscious letting go of the rational thought processes, the shift in consciousness to the Higher Self takes place naturally, without the need for the attention to be focused onto any other words or objects in order to induce a state of relaxation.

The following meditation can be practised at any time and for any duration. I would recommend twice daily to begin with, and for twenty to thirty minutes. It is best to meditate before meals, as the body can relax more easily if it is not actively digesting food.

Preparation for Meditation

Sit in an upright position. You can use an armchair if you wish, but sit with your back as straight as you can manage comfortably. Take a few deep breaths and feel yourself beginning to relax. Check your body for any areas of tension and just release them. Let the thoughts on the surface of your mind settle down for a minute or two.

Meditation

With your eyes open, begin by looking at the general area in front of you. Without focusing on anything in particular, keep your attention outwards on what the eyes can see. Notice any train of thought you are having and drop it. This is done by simply letting go of the thought. When you do this, it may feel like a release of tension, or alternatively a bit like to stopping short in the middle of a sentence. Where possible, resist the temptation to continue the old train of thought or pick up a new one.

Stopping the thought brings you into the

present moment, and you may immediately feel some pressure or discomfort somewhere in the body. This could be due either to feelings that were already there being brought into the awareness, or to fear of the unknown. There is no need to fear. Instead of letting the discomfort force you into more thinking, keep your attention firmly on the physical part of you that is feeling uncomfortable. Do not think about it but just feel it. Relax, and breathe into the discomfort, allowing yourself to fully experience it. This way you will dissolve it, thereby increasing your clarity of consciousness.

More thoughts will come, and may sometimes take over the mind completely for long periods. Do not get irritated when this loss of awareness happens - it is just one way that your body releases stress, and does not mean that the meditation is not working.

Each time you become aware that you are thinking:

(a) Drop the thought.

(b) Come into the Present Moment.

(c) Check inside yourself to see if there is

discomfort, and breathe into it until it is clear. As it begins to clear you may feel the desire to yawn or sigh. Do so if need be, but keep checking to see if the uncomfortable feeling has fully gone.

After you have been following this procedure for ten to fifteen minutes, or sooner if your eyes are getting tired, you can continue meditating with your eyes closed.

When you first close your eyes, you will notice the darkness, and then probably become aware of some further discomfort. This is because your attention is naturally turned inwards, once the visual images are withdrawn. Just follow the same procedure as before, breathing into the discomfort until it is cleared, keeping your attention in the Here and Now and letting go of the thought processes when you become aware of them.

Finishing Off

When you have completed the time set aside for meditating, you can start to prepare for coming back to the world of activity. This may take up to two minutes, depending on how deep a state of relaxation you have reached. After a short time you can slowly open your eyes, and begin to move and stretch the limbs. The meditation is now complete.

Further Points Concerning the Meditation

(1)   People sometimes have difficulty at first in identifying areas of discomfort which occur in meditation as stress begins to be released. These areas can be anywhere, but are commonly located around the solar plexus, heart and throat. Such feelings may not be substantial, and will often move around. A common example is boredom, with a desire to keep looking at the time in the hope that the session will end soon. Here is a typical sign that there is discomfort which can, with a little practice, be physically located.

(2)   During the latter part of the meditation, you may find that your breathing slows down and becomes very shallow. This need not cause any concern; it is a good sign,

and just means that you are entering a deep state of relaxation. Some of the time you may feel that you are somewhere between being in the Present Moment, feeling the feelings inside, and having thoughts also going on in the background. This is normal and a sign that the meditation is working well. However, do not become complacent and neglect the procedure of constantly eliminating thoughts.

(3) Although none of the steps in this meditation should be difficult to understand, there are nevertheless many steps. Reading the description slowly onto a tape and then playing it back when you want to practise meditating may help you, but it may on the other hand interfere with the meditation. Therefore it might be better simply to study and become familiar with each of the steps in the meditation before starting to practise. Paying attention to detail is important. Meditation is simple and easy to get right if the instructions are directly

followed, but it is also very subtle and easy to get wrong if the directions are misinterpreted. When I first began to meditate, I was practising for over a year before I was checked by someone and discovered that, by a small adjustment, my experience could be greatly improved. The problem had been simply due to not listening properly to the instructions. So I would advise periodically rereading the description, even after you have established a routine.

(4) Meditation should be effortless; its purpose is just to *Be*. Although there are many instructions, once you are familiar with them, they can each be performed without any strain. If you feel you are making an effort at any time just let go and follow the instructions in a very simple and straightforward way.

(5) Keeping your eyes open for the first part of the meditation is a deviation from the way of most techniques, and deserves some explanation. The reasons are twofold.

Firstly, learning to transfer consciousness into the Higher Mind with the eyes open will initiate a habit that can be used in daily life, rather than always associating a state of Higher Consciousness with having the eyes closed. Secondly, it is easier to stay *Present* with the eyes open during the early part of the meditation, because the visual images help keep the attention focused at a time when the mind is more active. Then, when the mind has had some time to settle down and the eyes are closed, the body can enter a deeper state of relaxation.

(6) Because the changes brought about by meditation in one's personality and quality of life occur gradually, you may not notice them occurring in yourself. Often it is other people who will notice the changes in you, particularly those who see you only occasionally.

(7) There are short-term effects and long-term effects. If, for instance, you sit down to meditate in an agitated state after a hard

day, you may afterwards feel refreshed and calm, and therefore enjoy the evening more; but that one session has not substantially changed you. On a day to day basis, you may feel calmer and more in control of your life, but the really deep rooted changes take place after months and years of practice. For this reason it is a mistake to think that meditation should be used as a problem solver, reserved only for times of stress. The key to change is long-term consistent practice.

(8) In this meditation the strength of one's intentions are important, in addition to the mere following of the instructions. The desire to release the thoughts and to focus the attention in the Present Moment will help the process. (In this respect some other forms of meditation differ, for instance those involving the mechanical repetition of a word or mantra).

(9) Because meditation may at times be very enjoyable, and you may get onto a plane of pleasant thoughts, it is sometimes tempting

to drop the procedures and allow yourself to keep thinking those thoughts that you are enjoying. This is a mistake, as you are then depriving yourself of the opportunity to go deeper into the meditation.

(10) The practice of meditation should be committed. It is unwise to think in terms of trying out meditation for a while to see if it works for you. With this attitude you will inevitably hit a rough patch where you are releasing stress continuously for a number of sessions, decide it is not working, and give up practising. I have met so many people who have taken up meditation and drifted away from the practice; nearly all have regretted not staying with it. Meditation should be judged over a reasonably long period, say six months. If after this time you feel that you have not benefited from the practice, you would then be justified in giving up and perhaps trying some other method.

(11) Those already practising some other technique of meditation have the choice to

continue with that method, swop for the one given here, or find some way to combine the two. The method outlined here is specifically designed to assist one in the practice of living in the Present Moment. Every technique has its own area of specialty, and affects the consciousness in a slightly different way. Your intuition is ultimately the best guide as to which method will suit your needs at each step along the way.

(12) The goal of meditation is to enter the Higher Conscious Mind, i.e. the Mind of God. We begin to achieve this as our mind starts to settle. However, this is not fully achieved until we are completely without thought. This is a state of *Pure Consciousness,* and one where a feeling of total bliss is experienced. The state of relaxation here is so deep that the breathing almost slows down to a standstill. In the early stages of meditation, it is rare to enter this state, and it usually only comes momentarily. But there are times when we

recognise its approach, even if we do not experience it in its purest form. As we continue meditating, we become more and more aware of how near or how far we are from this state of being.

(13) The practice of meditation should be regular. It should be so automatic as to be done in the same unquestioning way you brush your teeth. Before breakfast and before supper are generally considered good times to meditate. Once you have established a routine, do not look for results. There are times when you may feel it has been a very pleasant, even blissful experience - others when it has seemed uncomfortable, or dull and boring. In the same way that we breathe in and out, there are cycles where you will be reaching into higher levels of awareness, alternating with times when there seems to be a never ending mountain of stress to be cleared. Just trust in the process that all is working for the good, and the stages you are going through are those that you need, in your

present stage of development. Remember, we are all starting with different stress levels, and for some of us there is a great deal of this to be cleared. On the one hand this might sound intimidating, but on the other, it is all the more reason to begin the journey towards the Light of Higher Consciousness.

Living in the Presence

Having reached the point in meditation of being able to make contact with God, the Higher Consciousness, the next stage is to enter this conscious state during the remaining part of our waking day. People often find, even after years of practice, that no matter how profound their experience of meditation has been, as soon as they enter activity again, they become lost in the meanderings of the rational mind. Given that we may spend perhaps an hour a day in total meditating, it is a pity to lose the opportunity to be in contact with the Higher Self for the remaining fifteen or so waking hours we have left.

Living in the Present, meaning in essence *"Living in the Presence of God"*, is the direction in which we are all ultimately evolving. Life presents an endless variety of situations to stimulate our desires and fears, until we eventually come to realise that there must be a way to climb off this wheel that seems to lead somewhere, but actually just keeps going round and round. If life can be seen as a play, then to act on the stage of this "Wheel of Illusions" is fine so long as we are enjoying the performance. The problems arise when we become so caught up in our individual dramas that we lose the awareness of the part we are playing, and unhappiness inevitably follows. Becoming centred in the Higher Consciousness allows us to play the "Game of Life" without letting it take us over, so that it remains an enjoyable experience. And so, as we become less bound by our thinking minds, the burden of living becomes ever lighter.

Bringing the reality experienced in meditation into the rest of life not only accelerates the effects of meditation but transforms one's whole feeling about being alive. Being *"In This Body"* is for most people rarely a pleasurable experience, or they would not be constantly escaping into diversionary activities. "Staying Present" during normal daily activity brings a greater awareness of the physical body, and the pleasure of just being in contact with one's senses.

One's ability to enter the "Presence" and

then keep increasing the time spent there, depends directly on the degree of dedication one has. The Biblical passage: "Seek and ye shall find: knock and it shall be opened unto you" (St. Matthew 7:7) is very apt. Having sought and found a method of opening the door (of consciousness), it is necessary to keep knocking until the door gradually opens. It does happen, but success depends directly on perseverance. The method itself is easy, but results do not always come quickly. If they did everyone would long ago have reached the state we are aspiring to.

The first stage of practising "Being Present" is the hardest. After a period of regular practice, you will find there are certain activities performed in a typical day, such as taking a bath or walking the dog, which will automatically remind you to give attention to being "In the Moment". Before this happens, the process of becoming fully conscious may at times seem tedious. In fact it is not as tedious as it first appears, but there is a danger that you may lose interest before having the chance to gather some momentum.

It is often the case that thinking about

performing some task, like for instance getting up in the morning, is far more unpleasant than performing the task itself. This is also the case with entering Present Time Consciousness. Here, we often become so attached to our thoughts that the idea of dropping them is abhorrent to us. We imagine that without our thoughts we will feel lost and uncomfortable. The actuality is that when we do let them go, the discomfort that we feel is much less than we had anticipated. The discomfort only comes, because some of our inner tension has risen to the surface of our awareness. This usually subsides quite quickly, and we are left in a much more peaceful, pleasant and aware state than before. Far from being lost, we are releasing the lower self and beginning to find our True Self.

To enter and maintain a state of "Being in the Present Moment" while physically active, one can use a method similar to that used for the meditation already described. There are, however, some differences depending on the level of demand that the current activity is making on one's attention. For instance, if you are sitting in an airport lounge waiting for a plane to take off, the method of staying in the present would be virtually the same as that for meditation, as very little would be required of your attention except to occasionally glance at the clock to make sure you do not miss your flight. By contrast, if you are driving a car in heavy traffic, much of your attention is needed to control the car and respond to the ever changing road conditions, so the simple rules of meditation cannot in this instance fully apply.

To first enter the "Presence" requires a moment of conscious awareness. We all get these moments from time to time - initially when you start practising these exercises it may be only a few times a day, when this consciousness of *"Here I Am"* comes to you. Normally people are not very comfortable with these moments of consciousness, and immediately return to a previous train of thought or search for a new one. For the purpose of "Staying Present", when this moment of awareness comes to you, just *Stay With It.* You may at first think "I am here, now", but then let that thought go. Do not be tempted to think any thoughts, but keep releasing them. Keep letting go of thoughts as you feel them arise, and at the same time feel the physical feelings that come up in the body, which again will often be found in the solar plexus, chest and throat areas. This is the same process of clearing out the inner tensions of the past that was used in meditation. Keeping the attention centred on the feelings as they arise will help to stop the mind from diverting to other thoughts, in order to escape the discomfort of these feelings.

Keep with you a sense of being open, that is, open to all experience that the bodily senses present to you. This includes not only the feelings of inner tensions just mentioned, but also all the other sensations - the sounds you hear, the general sense of vision, the sensation of breathing in and out, the feeling of the air on your face and the clothes against your skin, and even the sensation of the blood running through your veins. Do not think about these sensations, but just let them come to your awareness, to the extent you are able.

The final part of the exercise is to give full attention to the activity at hand. Doing all of this together may sound like an impossible juggling act, but it is not so difficult as one might imagine. It is only difficult when you use the rational mind to try and analyse all the things you are doing. If you do not think about all your bodily sensations, but just feel them, it is quite easy. These sensations are there anyway, and the only thing that prevents you from feeling them is the activity of your mind. So, from this natural state of an awareness of the senses, it is quite easy to then give your attention simultaneously to whatever you are doing. If you catch yourself thinking about something else, for instance what you are going to have for supper, let it go, and keep coming back into the present moment. If you are performing a physical task, keep your attention on where the surfaces meet, which is where the activity is taking place. So if, for instance, you are peeling a potato, your attention will be where the knife meets the potato skin.

Periodically come back to an awareness of the body to see if any new feelings have come up that need to be cleared. You will know instinctively if you are successfully staying *Present and Conscious.*

Be willing to perform just one task at a time. It is not necessary to be thinking about one thing while doing another, although many of us live with a lurking anxiety that there is always something that we should be thinking about. This is an illusion. Certain problems do need to be thought out, but we create further problems for ourselves by agonising about decisions that we have already made. This way we carry tension from one situation to the next. If we reach a conclusion on a topic and then let go of the subject mentally, we are free to give our full attention to the next task that presents itself. Usually if any further adjustment is required to the first decision, the Higher Mind will present it to us at some convenient moment.

Given that we are not yet fully enlightened, we should not expect to enter Present Time Consciousness as a perfect state - that is to say, although we may have a marked sense of inner stillness and a consciousness of being present *Here and Now,* there are also a few thoughts coming and going somewhere in the background. Sooner or later these background thoughts tend to dominate again, and the state of "Presence" is lost until the next time.

On entering the state of *Being Present* one can notice that it has certain characteristics. Physically there may be a sense of slight pressure in the the forehead area - a pleasant sensation a little like being under water. It has been variously described in such terms as "A Feeling of Numbness in the Head", and also as being "In the Thickness of the Moment". Once the Light of Consciousness has dispersed some of the inner tensions, we are gradually brought into a space where there is a pleasant peaceful sense of detachment and a feeling that all is well. The world we now see looks new and different, and there is a sense of wonder, comparable to playing a Virtual Reality computer game for the first time. It bears some resemblance to being intoxicated, but here you are in complete control of all your faculties, and far from suffering from a hangover, the after-effects are refreshing and energising.

In order to progress, it is necessary to keep increasing the number of times and the duration spent in this "Presence". Once you have got over the first stages of resistance with such thoughts as "This won't work for me" or "This is boring" or "This requires too much hard work" or "I haven't time for all this", then just persevering with the practice of being "In the Moment" will automatically bring its own rewards.

Coming "Into the Moment" can happen in two different ways:

The first is spontaneously, where for no apparent reason the awareness comes to you that you are *Here, Present, Now.* This may happen as little as two or three times a day when you first begin the practice of Being Present, but you will notice a dramatic increase in this number as time passes.

The second way is habit. You will find as you practise that at certain specific times, it becomes quite easy to enter the consciousness of the Present Moment. If you practise regularly entering this state while, to take the earlier example, peeling potatoes, then it will eventually become a habit for you to enter (or think of entering) this state automatically each time you come to perform this task. As you persevere with the practice, more and more activities start to fall into this category of habits which trigger the practice of being conscious.

You may find that certain times are more conducive than others for practising being Here and Now. Some of these may include the following:

(1) Taking a walk is one of the easiest ways to enter and maintain a state of Being Present, preferably in a quiet environment and on a fine day (a biting wind, for example would tend to distract the mind). The rhythmic movement of walking makes it easy for one to allow the Higher Mind to take over, so that one can observe oneself in motion without thinking about it. Additionally, when you let the thoughts go while walking, you can enter a state of watching the scenery slowly passing by as if you were looking at a film in 3D. The outer environment while walking is stimulating enough to hold the attention, but not necessarily stimulating enough to demand that we think about it, so there is a nice balance that allows you to stay "In the Present".

(2) Jogging, and other exercises of the more strenuous variety, offer a greater challenge to someone trying to stay "Present", because the more energetic exercises tend to stir up the tensions that are stored in the body. It is naturally harder to maintain

one's attention at this time, because more tension means more discomfort, and therefore more tendency for the rational mind to escape into thinking. On the other hand, there is an opportunity to release a greater amount of tension through the conscious awareness. It is interesting to note that some people find jogging to be a boring exercise (which presumably relates to the discomfort they feel), while others can become quite addicted to it. Many seem to find that after jogging for some time, they enter a very peaceful mental state. It would seem that such exercises bring enough tension to the surface that a certain amount can be released, even without making an attempt at being "Present"; but this is not to say that maintaining conscious awareness would not improve the effect.

(3) Any situation where you have to wait is an opportunity to enter the Present Moment. The times which are normally so tedious, such as waiting at traffic lights, supermarkets, or doctors' waiting rooms, can thus be turned around so that each

situation becomes a challenge to stay present and conscious for as long as possible.

(4) Driving a car can be a very good time to practise living "In the Present". Having learnt to drive, the whole action of driving becomes so automatic that one can observe oneself going through the motions while hardly having to think at all. On long journeys particularly, it can sometimes be quite easy to slip into *Present Time Consciousness* and observe the scenery passing by while, like an automatic pilot, the Higher Mind takes over the controls of the car. Giving attention to the scenery does not mean that you have lost consciousness of driving the car. It is a simultaneous consciousness of both the driving and the scenery. While the mind is not distracted by other thoughts, awareness can be maintained on all levels.

(5) All kinds of repetitive tasks offer an opportunity to come into the Present Moment because, generally speaking, they do not occupy the mind. This is why they are considered boring, but this can in fact

be turned to advantage by feeling into the physical sensation of the boredom, and then giving full and "non-thinking" attention to the activity at the place where the surfaces meet.

The more you practise living in "The Presence" the more you will find new ways to make it work for you. The times set aside for meditation will greatly enhance your practice. As mentioned previously, a minimum of twenty minutes twice a day is recommended, but there are also many other times during the day when you can usually find a few spare minutes or even just a few moments in which to "come to" and be in contact with your Higher Self. Such times would include the period before going to sleep and after waking up, and any opportunity to give the mind a rest between activities. Stopping for such a break between one activity and the next is a very good way of avoiding the tension build-up that occurs during a working day. Another suggestion is to develop the habit of doing nothing occasionally - it can be very rewarding, in contrast to our usual conditioning which leads us to believe that we should always be doing something to justify our existence.

Being in God's Presence is a beautiful state. I know this, only through my own experience of the practices I have endeavoured to describe. I can observe that as I continue with these practices, a process is occurring whereby, gradually, the clarity of my state of being improves. I believe this state of being is accessible to all people, requiring only perseverance - a willingness to keep trying in the belief that it is there to be reached. And in the end there is no trying - just the realisation that the Presence of God is *Here, Now.*

Happiness

Our prime motivation in life is to be happy – few would dispute this – in fact all action seems to spring from this first impulse. So it might be said that the search for God is in essence a search for happiness. On the other hand, while it is appears that everyone is seeking happiness, it is equally apparent that not everyone is seeking God. And as we look around at the majority of people in their varied existences, it would seem that happiness has proved an elusive goal; which begs a few questions: can the search for happiness be divorced from seeking contact with the inner core of our being – that which links us to God? Can we pursue happiness directly as a state of being, or is happiness dependent purely on circumstances? What, in fact, do we actually mean by happiness, and why do we have such difficulty in attaining this state?

The dictionary defines the word "Happy"

firstly as "Glad" and secondly as "Content". Already we can see two slightly different meanings. In the sense of being glad, happiness comes as a result of something happening, for example "I am happy (or glad) that I've just passed my exams". It has a quality of excitement and is short-lived – experience tells us that gladness comes and goes. Contentment, on the other hand, is a state that we relax into: "I am happy (or content) just to be here". Contentment is the more passive aspect of happiness, and so has the potential for greater permanence. But is contentment capable of giving the same degree of fulfilment as the more active forms of happiness? Or does contentment merely imply a watered down version of happiness, the sort of thing we might settle for when old age has diminished our capacity for the more intense forms of pleasure?

To answer this question, it is necessary to get inside the real meaning of happiness. Leaving aside dictionary definitions, what we are concerned about is how good we feel, and over what period this feeling is sustained.

Without the help of science, it is very hard to measure happiness – to know how happy we are now in comparison to some previous time. We have to rely on memory, which is not always reliable. Looking back on a sun drenched holiday we forget just how hot it really was, how thirsty we were, and how the mosquitoes kept us awake. And without science it is also impossible to know how happy we are in comparison to anyone else, as there is no way of knowing how another person feels except on a very superficial level.

Technology has recently made significant strides in the area of measuring happiness. Different chemicals produced by the body have been shown to correspond with different forms of happiness. The anticipation of a pleasing result, for instance, produces a different chemical than the euphoric realisation of a goal. And when a person is happy, certain areas of the brain have been shown to become more active. So now it is possible to produce a computerised picture showing a person's overall state of well-being. Although the technology is yet at an early stage, several methods to improve this level of well-being have proved effective. Some of these would include such simple measures as: the setting of realistic goals, periodic reminders not to take life too seriously, taking up hobbies, and finding ways to create laughter.

Feeling good is largely dependent on our making contact with the life force within us. This is true of the excitement kind, and also of the contentment kind. In essence, *To Feel Good Is To Feel Life.* This is our natural state, and if our consciousness was clear and without interference, we would feel good all of the time.

But, of course, we do not feel good all of the time. Two factors, when present, can counteract the good feelings. The first of these is pain. Pain, as we know, makes us feel less good. It may be of the physical or emotional kind, and is sometimes unavoidable. Much of our emotional pain, however, is derived from thinking about painful situations that occurred in our past, or which might occur in our future. A lot of this pain is generated by excessive thinking, and so has the potential to be avoided.

The other factor which reduces our capacity to feel good is less easy to detect. It can be thought of as a smoke screen, which hangs over the consciousness much like a fog, and reduces the contact we have with our own life force. This smoke screen, which we all have to varying degrees, is produced by the rational mind creating "clouds" of thoughts and emotions which, as we have already seen, build up and prevent the clear light of consciousness from shining through. The feelings experienced as a result of the smoke screen are not quite strong enough to be called pain but would be described more as a dull sensation, or one of confusion. If enough of these "clouds" build up they may lead to depression.

Unhappiness is easy enough to understand. Something unpleasant happens, our mind interprets and produces an emotion which is felt as a disturbance in the body. Whatever joy we are experiencing at being alive is overridden by this disturbance, and we say we are unhappy. Equally, the aforementioned smoke screen can produce feelings of unhappiness if it is dense enough to cut us off from our life force.

Happiness, of the kind we are most familiar with, is usually stimulated by something happening – an event which makes us feel safe, secure, loved, excited – that feeling that life is good, or about to get better. For a period of time a chemical reaction occurs in the body that brings us into a state of euphoria, a heightened awareness – full contact with the life force. Then, when the event passes or we become accustomed to whatever new conditions it has brought, the body settles back to its original state and the happiness subsides.

But happiness need not occur only as a result of outside stimulation. If the life force within were completely unhampered by "clouds" of thoughts, inner tensions, or emotions, then we would be permanently in *"Bliss Consciousness"* – the state the mystical traditions refer to as "Enlightenment". This is happiness in its truest form. It is our natural state, and one of perfect peace and contentment. Perfect happiness, therefore, could be said to be a total lack of unhappiness. This, on the one hand might seem obvious, but it points to a less obvious conclusion; which is that *the only way towards true and permanent happiness is through the elimination of unhappiness.* This turns the tables on the common view of life, which is to try and grab hold of as much happiness as possible – a pursuit which we know through experience does not bring enduring results.

And so it becomes clear that we can seek happiness in two ways – one through manipulating the outer environment; and the other through working on ourselves, not only to improve our day to day responses to whatever life presents, but also to clear out all the resident unhappiness that lives inside us.

Since the desire for happiness is at the root of so many of our decisions in life, it is vital to be clear about which decisions will bring us which kinds of happiness. In fact most people's decisions invariably revolve around factors outside of themselves to "make" them happy – factors which may be short–term influences or long-term influences. Because they are so common, everyone has some awareness of short-term influences and the fact that they cannot bring lasting results. We know that a good meal will only bring satisfaction for a short while, or even that the new car we are saving up for will bring excitement only for a limited period. The form of happiness that people usually think of as long-term, might be better described as "medium-term", yet is the kind the majority spend a lifetime trying to achieve. It is seen as that most difficult balancing act of getting everything right – good health, an interesting job, financial security, a fulfilling relationship. But even the few who realise most of these goals, often discover that true contentment still eludes them. Discontent remains somewhere within, and improved circumstances can often leave a person feeling disappointedly unchanged.

This is not to attach any blame to looking for fulfilment outside of ourselves. It is in our nature to seek happiness in the outer environment. Getting the circumstances right in our lives does help us to feel more safe and secure, and as we strive to achieve this balance so we learn increasingly to live in harmony with our surroundings. This is good, but if we look no deeper than this, our happiness is dependent on the whims of an ever changing environment. A loved one dies and we take years to recover the sense of loss; or we lose our job and enter a period of decline. Fluctuations in our state of being are unavoidable, but it is important to be able to return quickly to a state of equilibrium and carry on.

There are those who say that the way to happiness is through giving to others. This way we forget about our own troubles, while at the same time feeling good that we are contributing something of benefit to the lives of those less fortunate. This is fine in principle, so long as the giving stems from our natural inclinations, and therefore seeks no rewards. If giving is turned into a project whereby, at the back of our mind somewhere we are hoping for a result, then we become disappointed and even bitter if our giving does not bear fruit. Giving becomes unconditional (or free) only when our consciousness is full and clear and therefore in harmony with the world around us. Then our desires and actions are always to promote harmony wherever we see the opportunity.

If we are serious about making happiness a permanent reality for ourselves, and not just a whim of circumstance, then we come back to the point that *Our True Nature* **IS** *Bliss Consciousness* (the purest form of happiness), and to experience this, we must get rid of all the tension, stress, and unhappy emotions which are obscuring it. These negative emotions have accumulated in the past and comprise the legacy which we carry with us in the present. We need not necessarily concern ourselves with how they got here, but just that we wish to be clear of them.

The pathway towards achieving happiness through the elimination of unhappiness must involve ways to clear the consciousness. It should therefore include such practices as meditation, and "Living in the Here and Now". Whatever methods one might choose to make use of for the journey, finding a pathway towards Full Consciousness, the realisation of the God within, is the only option if one is intent on pursuing happiness as a permanent reality. The happiness which we seek in the outer world can only be a pale shadow by comparison.

First and foremost, to be happy means to be fully alive and therefore fully conscious. This is because *Life and Consciousness are One and the Same;* they both have their root in the Eternal Being, and that, after all, is the place where happiness resides.

Conclusion

In adopting any philosophy or related set of practices, there is often a danger of becoming limited by that particular belief system. When one finds a new way of looking at life that seems to make more sense or bring greater fulfilment, it is tempting to attach oneself to that new system and look no further. Many, if not most religious sects encourage this practice through claiming a virtual monopoly on the truth i.e. that their way is the best, or perhaps even the only way to God. This approach can lead to a sense of stagnation, as one's natural inclination to explore new avenues of thinking becomes frustrated.

The purpose of this book was not to offer a *"Best"* way, but just a way - to view God as something within oneself rather than as some remote external figure-head, and to explore a few techniques of making contact with this Higher Self from which we have become so separated. The techniques used are not intended as a comprehensive package, but merely as a starting point from which further techniques may be added or even substituted as found appropriate.

Where spiritual growth is concerned, we have no way of knowing in advance which developmental aids will best suit our individual needs. Given the huge variety of techniques available, it is unlikely we shall find our individual "best" one first time around. Additionally, as we change and grow, so naturally do our requirements, and that which works well for us today may need updating in a few years time. So some degree of experimentation is needed in order to find our optimum growth pathway. One needs firstly to identify what seems a good form of practice, secondly to take whatever steps are needed to begin practising; finally to persevere until such time as a better course of action presents itself. Chopping and changing from one system to another is no better than becoming locked into a particular system: so it is necessary to find a balance. If, for instance, a method of meditation seems appealing, you might decide to try it for six months: then if no tangible results can be seen within this period, you would be justified in searching elsewhere.

It is easy to delay the practical aspect of the search for God. There are so many diversions in life that appear on the surface to be more attractive options. Some of these can even take the form of disguises - pretending to lead us to God, but in reality just stimulating more mental activity. For every person actually putting their beliefs into practice, there are tens of others merely philosophising - an enjoyable pastime, but as we have seen, such activity of the mind only takes us further from our Source of Being.

It is also easy, having made some progress, to then give up the search for God. It happens frequently that people either drift away from a practice such as meditation, say they cannot make the time, or find some other excuse. Too much is at stake for these excuses to be valid, except in exceptional circumstances. Contacting our Creator, the Source of Life, has such benefits, while drifting away from this Source has such potential losses, that we cannot afford to let so called "Practicalities of Life" stand in the way of this contact. If the desire is strong enough, a way will always be found. This desire for contact with God grows ever stronger as practice brings increasing knowledge of its value. Once we are aware of this truth, we carry the responsibility for that knowledge: for now the power to shape our destiny is placed squarely in our own hands.